The

HALLOWEEN
TRIVIA
Game Book

What you need

- This book!
- 2-6 players
- Scoring method (Pen and paper, or smartphone)

How to play

Choose a person to keep score.

General trivia questions are worth 1, 2 or 3 points based on difficulty. The youngest player reads the first question to the player directly to his or her right. If the player answers correctly, he or she earns the number of points for that question. (Correct answers can be found on the page that follows each question.) The youngest player passes the book to the person on his or her left, who then asks the next question to the youngest player. Continue moving the book around your group in this fashion.

If only two players, simply pass the book back and forth. You may also choose to play in two teams instead of as individuals.

If a player lands on a bonus round page, that person or team will have an opportunity to earn up to 5 points. Read all instructions aloud when landing on a bonus round page. The question reader should keep track of correct answers in a bonus round, and tally the points for the scorekeeper.

The player or team with the most points at the end wins. You may choose to play the entire book. For a shorter round, elect to end the game on page 50 or page 100, and pick up from there next time.

2
POINTS

QUESTION

What Halloween candy
was originally called
chicken feed?

ANSWER

Candy corn

3
POINTS

QUESTION

What horror movie
received 10 Academy Award
nominations in 1974?

"The Exorcist"

3 POINTS

QUESTION

Which U.S. state produces the most pumpkins?

ANSWER

Illinois

2
POINTS

QUESTION

What percent of parents in the United States admit to stealing candy from their children's Halloween bags?

90 percent

2

POINTS

QUESTION

Steven Spielberg incorporated two of his childhood fears in the 1982 movie "Poltergeist." One was a tree outside the window with long branches. What was the other?

ANSWER

A clown doll

POINTS

"Starlight" was the original name of what Michael Jackson song that is often played around Halloween?

ANSWER

"Thriller"

1
POINT

QUESTION

True or false: According to the National Retail Federation, about 25 percent of Americans will carve a pumpkin for Halloween.

False. About 44 percent will.

1
POINT

QUESTION

True or false: Michael Keaton appears as the title character in the movie "Beetlejuice" for only 17 minutes.

ANSWER

True!

2
POINTS

QUESTION

What is
Samhainophobia?

ANSWER

A fear of Halloween

BONUS
Round!

BONUS Round!

UP TO

5 POINTS

Name the top five most popular candy choices in the United States for Halloween, according to research done in 2021 and 2022.
You may take five guesses total.
(One point per correct answer for a maximum of 5 points.)

Reese's Peanut Butter Cups

Kit Kat

Skittles

M&M's

Snickers

2
POINTS

QUESTION

In the original "Halloween" movie, the Michael Myers character wore a $2 mask of what actor that was spray-painted white?

William Shatner
(The mask was a modified
Captain Kirk mask from the TV
series "Star Trek.")

QUESTION

What was The Munsters' address?

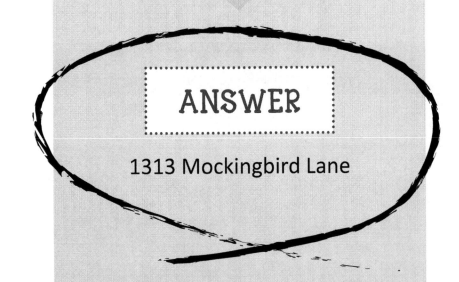

ANSWER

1313 Mockingbird Lane

3 POINTS

QUESTION

Who sang the original
"Monster Mash?"

ANSWER

Bobby Pickett

QUESTION

The Academy Awards'
Oscar statuette inspired the
shape of what character from
a classic horror movie?

"The Creature from the
Black Lagoon"

2

POINTS

QUESTION

Why do some people wear
their clothes inside out
on Halloween?

The superstitious believe they will see a witch at midnight.

2 POINTS

QUESTION

What comedian inspired Jordan Peele to write the movie "Get Out"?

ANSWER

Eddie Murphy

2 POINTS

QUESTION

Where does the phrase "Double, double toil and trouble" come from?

ANSWER

William Shakespeare's
"Macbeth"

QUESTION

Drew Barrymore auditioned for "Poltergeist" but was instead cast in what other Stephen Spielberg film?

"E.T. the Extra-Terrestrial"

2 POINTS

QUESTION

Prior to pumpkins, which
root vegetable did the Irish
and Scottish carve
on Halloween?

ANSWER

Turnips

1
POINT

QUESTION

Is a pumpkin a fruit or
a vegetable?

ANSWER

A fruit! (It has seeds.)

BONUS
Round!

BONUS Round!

UP TO

4
POINTS

Some U.S. states have a most popular Halloween candy that is different from the national top five favorites. Read each statement below aloud. The guesser will name the candy that is most favored for each state or group of states.
(One point per correct answer for a maximum of 4 points.)

Residents in Delaware, Michigan, and Texas favor these fruity square candies.	**Starburst**
Florida and Nebraska prefer this galaxy-themed candy bar.	**Milky Way**
In Kentucky, residents like this candy bar, which is also slang for someone who is clumsy.	**Butterfinger**
Montana and Vermont like this spicy candy.	**Hot Tamales**

QUESTION

Who wrote the horror classic
"Frankenstein"?

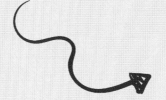

ANSWER

Mary Shelley

2 POINTS

Every Halloween, Charlie Brown helps his friend Linus wait for what character to appear?

ANSWER

The Great Pumpkin

2
POINTS

QUESTION

In what country is
Transylvania located?

ANSWER

Romania

3
POINTS

QUESTION

Which U.S. First Lady is said
to haunt the White House
rose garden?

Dolley Madison

2
POINTS

Dan Aykroyd co-wrote the
movie "Ghostbusters" with
what other actor?

ANSWER

Harold Ramis

2
POINTS

QUESTION

In what U.S. state is it illegal
to dress up as a nun, priest, or
other religious figure
for Halloween?

ANSWER

Alabama

QUESTION

What item that you might find in your kitchen is used to scare vampires away?

ANSWER

Garlic

2
POINTS

QUESTION

What city hosts the world's
largest Halloween parade?

ANSWER

New York City

BONUS
Round!

BONUS Round!

UP TO

5
POINTS

Name the least five popular Halloween candies in the United States, according to 2021 data. You may take five total guesses. (One point for each correct answer for a maximum of 5 points.)

Candy corn

Circus peanuts

Hershey's Kisses

Smarties

Necco wafers

2 POINTS

QUESTION

In the movie "Mean Girls, Lindsay Lohan's character dresses up as whom to attend a Halloween party?

The Bride of Frankenstein

2
POINTS

QUESTION

What is the name
of the large pot that witches
use to make potions?

ANSWER

Cauldron

QUESTION

True or false: The first
"Paranormal Activity" movie
was released in 2000.

ANSWER

False.
It was released in 2007.

1
POINT

QUESTION

True or false: The movie
"Resident Evil" was originally
a video game.

True!

2
POINTS

QUESTION

What is the name
of Jodie Foster's character in
"The Silence of the Lambs?"

ANSWER

Clarice Starling

QUESTION

Movie killer Jason Voorhees wears a mask from what sport?

Hockey

2
POINTS

QUESTION

What U.S. football team
has a name inspired by
Edgar Allan Poe?

ANSWER

The Baltimore Ravens

2 POINTS

QUESTION

Fill in the missing word: Disney's Haunted Mansion ride starts with the host saying, "Welcome, foolish _____, to the Haunted Mansion."

ANSWER

Mortals

2 POINTS

QUESTION

What is the name of Neve
Campbell's character in the
movie "Scream?"

ANSWER

Sidney Prescott

2
POINTS

QUESTION

What was Stephen King's
first published novel?

ANSWER

"Carrie" (1973)

BONUS
Round!

BONUS Round!

UP TO

5
POINTS

Name the top five most popular Halloween costumes
for Google searches in 2022. You may take five guesses total.
(One point per correct answer for a maximum of 5 points.)

Witch

Spider-Man

Dinosaur

"Stranger Things" characters

Fairy

2 POINTS

QUESTION

What is the name of the killer in the "Saw" movie franchise?

ANSWER

Jigsaw

2 POINTS

QUESTION

Who directed the 1963
film "The Birds?"

ANSWER

Alfred Hitchcock

3 POINTS

QUESTION

What group of people originally associated black cats with witchcraft and bad luck, which led to them becoming a symbol for Halloween?

ANSWER

The Puritans

3
POINTS

QUESTION

In what year was Trick or Treat
for UNICEF founded?

ANSWER

1980

3
POINTS

QUESTION

"Halloween House" was the original title for what Disney Halloween movie?

ANSWER

"Hocus Pocus"

QUESTION

Why did people originally start dressing up in Halloween costumes?

ANSWER

To repel spirits

1

POINT

QUESTION

True or false: Most U.S. states do not require homeowners to disclose paranormal activity when selling their house.

True!

1 POINT

QUESTION

True or false: The average American spends about $50 on Halloween celebrations.

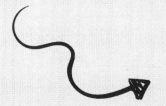

False. The average Americans
spends closer to $100
at Halloween.

2 POINTS

QUESTION

Who wrote the "The Legend of Sleepy Hollow"?

ANSWER

Washington Irving

2
POINTS

QUESTION

In which country did
Halloween originate?

ANSWER

Ireland

3 POINTS

QUESTION

How many Academy Awards nominations did the movie "Psycho" receive?

ANSWER

Four

3
POINTS

QUESTION

What classic horror film features the quote, "They're coming to get you, Barbara"?

ANSWER

"Night of the Living Dead"

2
POINTS

QUESTION

According to Zillow, what U.S. city is the best for trick-or-treating?

ANSWER

San Francisco

2
POINTS

QUESTION

What colors make up
Freddy Krueger's shirt in
"A Nightmare on Elm Street?"

ANSWER

Red and green

3 POINTS

QUESTION

Which actor turned down
the role of Max Dennison
in "Hocus Pocus"?

ANSWER

Leonardo DiCaprio

1 POINT

QUESTION

True or false: Bobbing for apples started as a courting ritual in Great Britain.

True! Each apple represented a potential suitor, and the bobber would try to bite the apple of the person she liked.

1
POINT

QUESTION

True or false:
There are eight ingredients
in a Butterfinger bar.

False!
There are 19 ingredients.

2
POINTS

QUESTION

What special ability does a person born on Halloween have, according to superstition?

ANSWER

The ability to
communicate with spirits

POINTS

QUESTION

Which witch does Dorothy accidentally kill at the beginning of "The Wizard of Oz?"

ANSWER

The Wicked Witch of the East

2
POINTS

QUESTION

What is a male witch
called?

ANSWER

A warlock

QUESTION

In which U.S. state does
"The Blair Witch Project"
take place?

ANSWER

Maryland

2
POINTS

QUESTION

What is the name of the hotel
Jack Torrance is hired to care
for in "The Shining?"

ANSWER

The Overlook Hotel

QUESTION

True or false: Americans spent more than $2 billion on Halloween candy in 2019.

ANSWER

True! They spent around
$2.6 billion.

POINT

QUESTION

True or false: Halloween is the
U.S. holiday with the highest
amount of candy sales.

ANSWER

False! Easter has higher
candy sales.

QUESTION

What is the name
of Dracula's sidekick?

ANSWER

Renfield

QUESTION

In the "Halloween" movie franchise, what is Michael Myers middle name?

ANSWER

Audry

3
POINTS

QUESTION

Who was the first First Lady
to decorate the White House
for Halloween?

ANSWER

Mamie Eisenhower (1958)

BONUS
Round!

BONUS Round!

UP TO

5
POINTS

There are several celebrities who were born on Oct. 31.
Read each celebrity description aloud. The guesser must name the
celebrity, who also happens to be born on Halloween.
One guess per description.
(One point for each correct answer for a maximum of 5 points.)

White rap artist who was a one-hit wonder in the 1990s.	**Vanilla Ice**
Actor who starred in rom-coms "My Best Friend's Wedding" and "The Wedding Date."	**Dermot Mulroney**
Member of the hip-hop group The Beastie Boys.	**Adam "Ad-Rock" Horovitz**
TV dad from "Little House on the Prairie."	**Michael Landon**
Actor who starred in "Planes, Trains, and Automobiles" and "Uncle Buck."	**John Candy**

3
POINTS

QUESTION

Which boy band used the mansion from "Casper" for one of their music videos?

143

ANSWER

The Backstreet Boys

QUESTION

Snickers and what other candy bar were the first to be offered in a "fun size"?

ANSWER

Milky Way

2
POINTS

How many takes did it take
to get the vomiting scene right
in The Exorcist?

ANSWER

One take

QUESTION

Which story originated the
Headless Horseman?

ANSWER

"The Legend of Sleepy Hollow"

2
POINTS

QUESTION

In Spain, Halloween is called
El Dia de los Muertos and lasts
for how many days?

ANSWER

Three

2
POINTS

QUESTION

What percentage of American adults say they will dress in costume for Halloween?

ANSWER

40 percent

3
POINTS

QUESTION

"House Ghosts" and "Sacred Sheetless" were early possible titles of what movie?

ANSWER

"Beetlejuice"

3
POINTS

QUESTION

In what country do children refer to dressing up for Halloween as guising?

ANSWER

Scotland

2
POINTS

QUESTION

What famous magician passed
away on Halloween?

ANSWER

Harry Houdini

2
POINTS

What is the name of the island
the gang visits in the 2002
Scooby-Doo movie?

Spooky Island

BONUS
Round!

BONUS Round!

UP TO

5
POINTS

Both are five statements about Halloween records
in the Guinness Book of World Records.
Decide whether each statement is true or false.
(One point for each correct answer for a maximum of 5 points.)

The world's heaviest pumpkin weighed just over 2,700 pounds.	**True!**
The world's largest collection of haunted dolls is located in Canada.	**False. It's located in Mexico.**
At a 2013 event in Spain, more than 1,600 people dressed as witches, setting a world record.	**True!**
The world's largest vampire gathering was achieved in the United Kingdom.	**True!**
A record-breaking 49 pumpkins were smashed in one minute in California.	**False. 52 pumpkins were smashed to set the record.**

3 POINTS

"The Babysitter Murders"
was the original title
of what movie?

"Halloween"

3
POINTS

QUESTION

According to ancient legend, seeing a spider on Halloween means what?

ANSWER

A spirit is watching over you,
or protecting you

QUESTION

What is the name of the large green ghost Ray first encounters in Ghostbusters?

ANSWER

Slimer

2 POINTS

QUESTION

In "The Ring," how long
do people have to live
after watching the cursed
video tape?

2
POINTS

QUESTION

Which item is banned in Hollywood during Halloween?

ANSWER

Silly String

2 POINTS

Which horror movie stars Jennifer Love Hewitt, Freddie Prinze Jr., Sarah Michelle Gellar and Ryan Phillippe?

"I Know What You Did
Last Summer"

3
POINTS

QUESTION

What was the profession
of William Morrison, the
inventor of cotton candy?

ANSWER

A dentist

2 POINTS

What is the name of the summer camp where "Friday the 13th" takes place?

ANSWER

Camp Crystal Lake

2 POINTS

QUESTION

What does a person see that turns them into a werewolf?

ANSWER

A full moon

3 POINTS

QUESTION

Who wrote the mystery novel titled Hallowe'en Party?

ANSWER

Agatha Christie

2
POINTS

QUESTION

Which U.S. president jokingly told a group of children that the White House was haunted by the ghost of Abraham Lincoln?

ANSWER

George H.W. Bush

POINTS

QUESTION

In 2020, there was a full moon on Halloween. What is the next year after that with a full moon on Halloween?

ANSWER

2039

2 POINTS

QUESTION

What killer dog did
Stephen King create?

ANSWER

"Cujo"

2 POINTS

QUESTION

What is a group
of witches called?

2
POINTS

QUESTION

From base to point, what is
the order of colors on
a traditional piece
of candy corn?

ANSWER

Yellow, orange, white

2
POINTS

QUESTION

Which of the following actors did not appear in "Interview with the Vampire": Brad Pitt, Antonio Banderas, Kiefer Sutherland or Tom Cruise?

ANSWER

Kiefer Sutherland

2 POINTS

QUESTION

What former model is known for throwing epic Halloween parties?

ANSWER

Heidi Klum

POINTS

QUESTION

In 2022, what was the most popular Halloween costume for pets?

ANSWER

A pumpkin

3
POINTS

QUESTION

What is phobophobia?

ANSWER

A fear of fear

3 POINTS

What horror movie was the
first American film ever to
show a toilet on screen?

Thank you!

The purchase of this book supported a small business. We hope you enjoyed it!